ID384668

ALBANY COUNTY
PUBLIC LIBRARY
Serving the Laramie Plains since 1887

Laramie, Wyoming 82070

PRESENTED BY

A Friend

CORN IS MAIZE
The Gift of the Indians

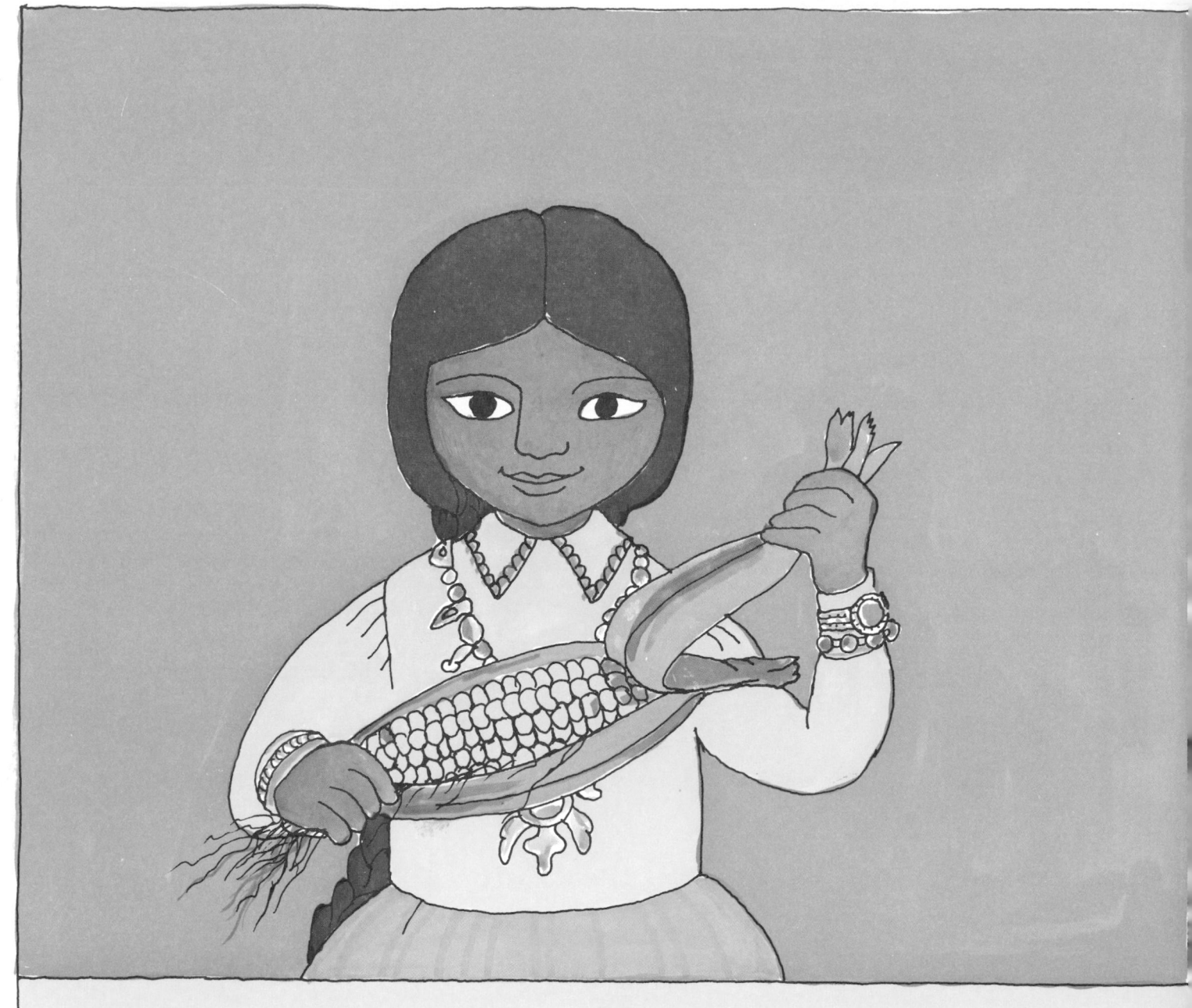

For Alicia, John, Darius, and Noel

Let's-Read-and-Find-Out Science®

CORN IS MAIZE
The Gift of the Indians

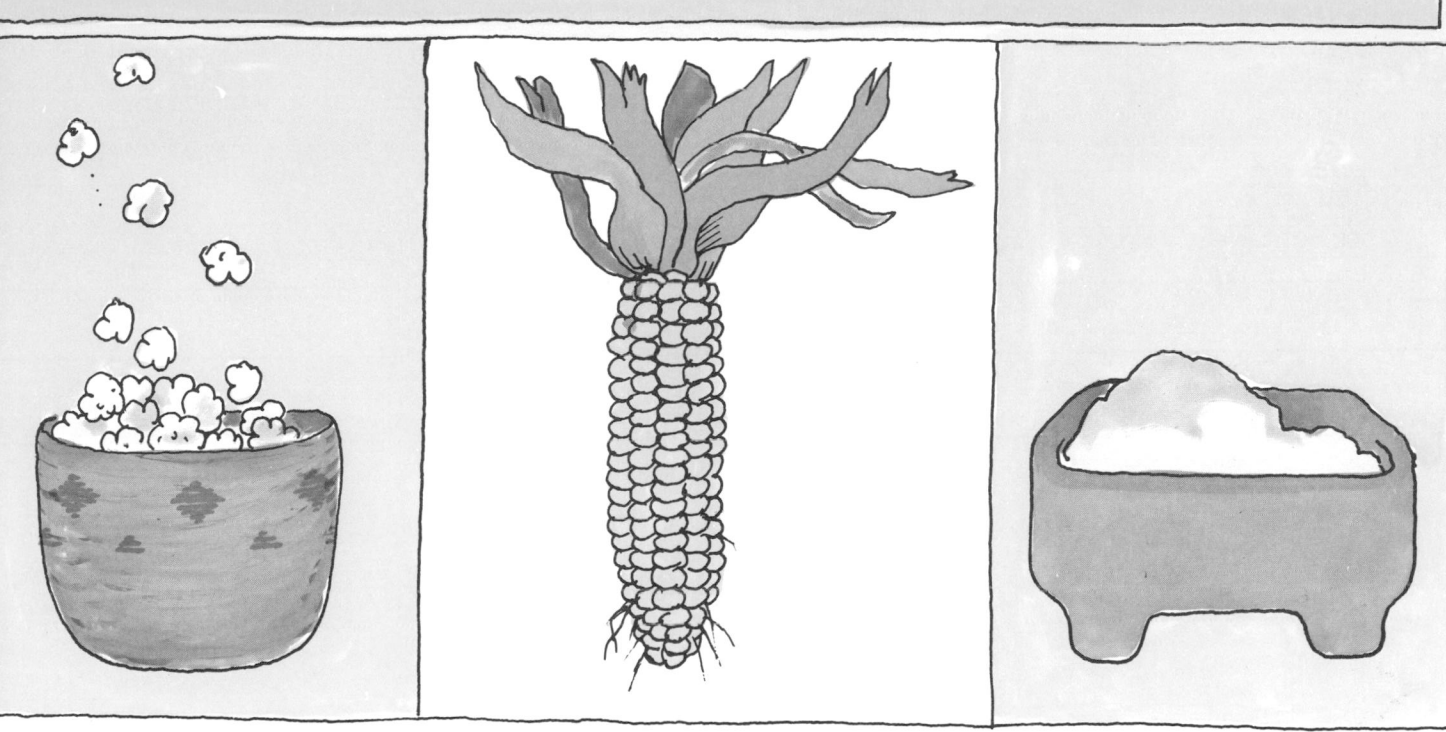

written and illustrated by
ALIKI

HarperCollins*Publishers*

The *Let's-Read-and-Find-Out Science* book series was originated by Dr. Franklyn M. Branley, Astronomer Emeritus and former Chairman of the American Museum–Hayden Planetarium, and was formerly co-edited by him and Dr. Roma Gans, Professor Emeritus of Childhood Education, Teachers College, Columbia University. Text and illustrations for each of the books in the series are checked for accuracy by an expert in the relevant field. For more information about Let's-Read-and-Find-Out Science books, write to HarperCollins Children's Books, 10 East 53rd Street, New York, NY 10022.

HarperCollins®, ☰®, Harper Trophy®and Let's Read-and-Find-Out Science®
are trademarks of HarperCollins Publishers Inc.

Library of Congress Cataloging-in-Publication Data
Aliki.
   Corn is maize.
   Summary: A simple description of how corn was discovered and
used by the Indians and how it came to be an important food
throughout the world.
   1. Maize—Juvenile literature.   2. Indians—Food—Juvenile
literature.   [1. Corn]   I. Title.
SB191.M2A584
633′.15′09   75-6928
ISBN 0-690-00975-5 (lib. bdg.)
ISBN 0-06-445026-0 (pbk.)

CORN IS MAIZE
The Gift of the Indians

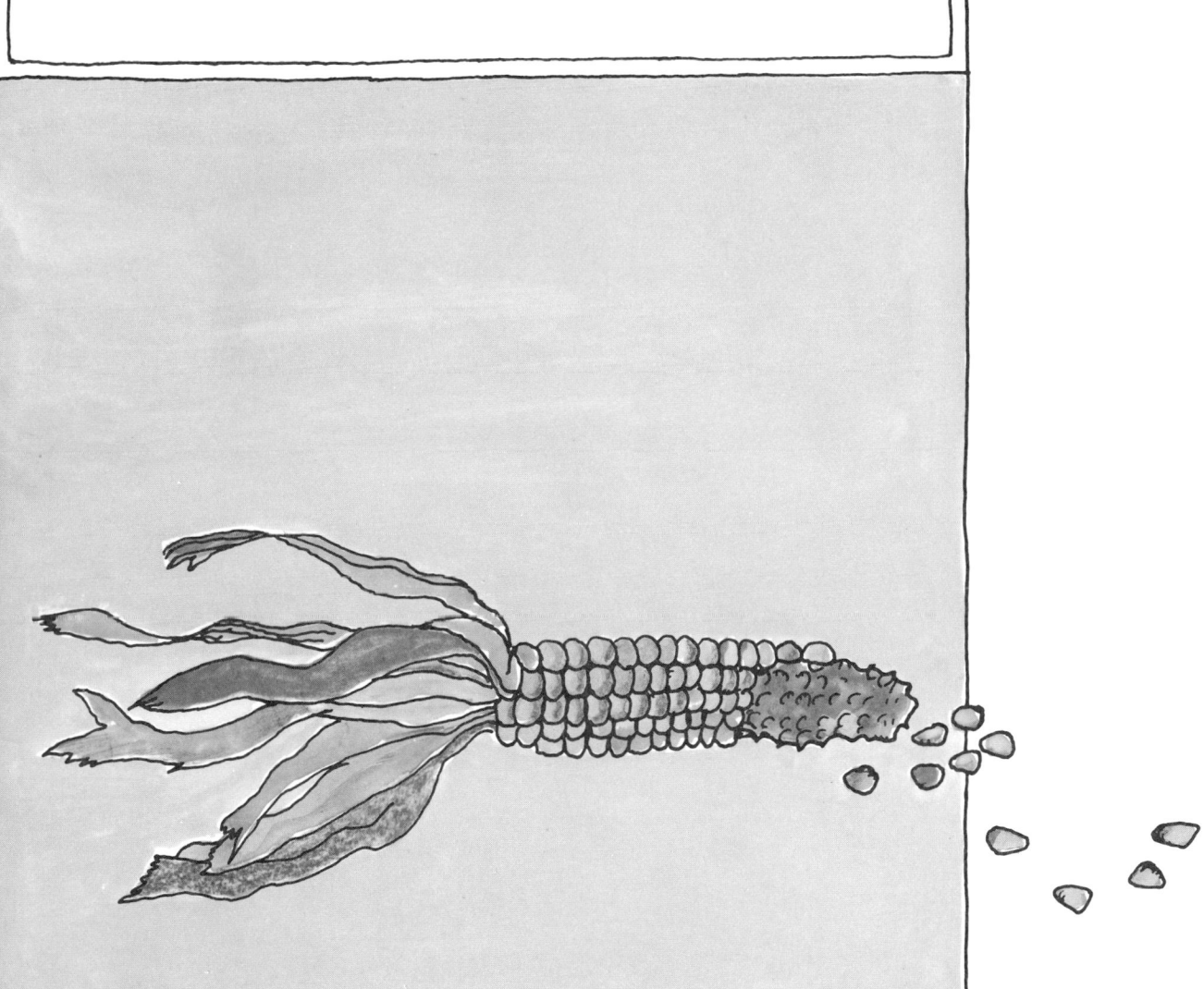

This is a kernel of corn.
It is a corn seed.

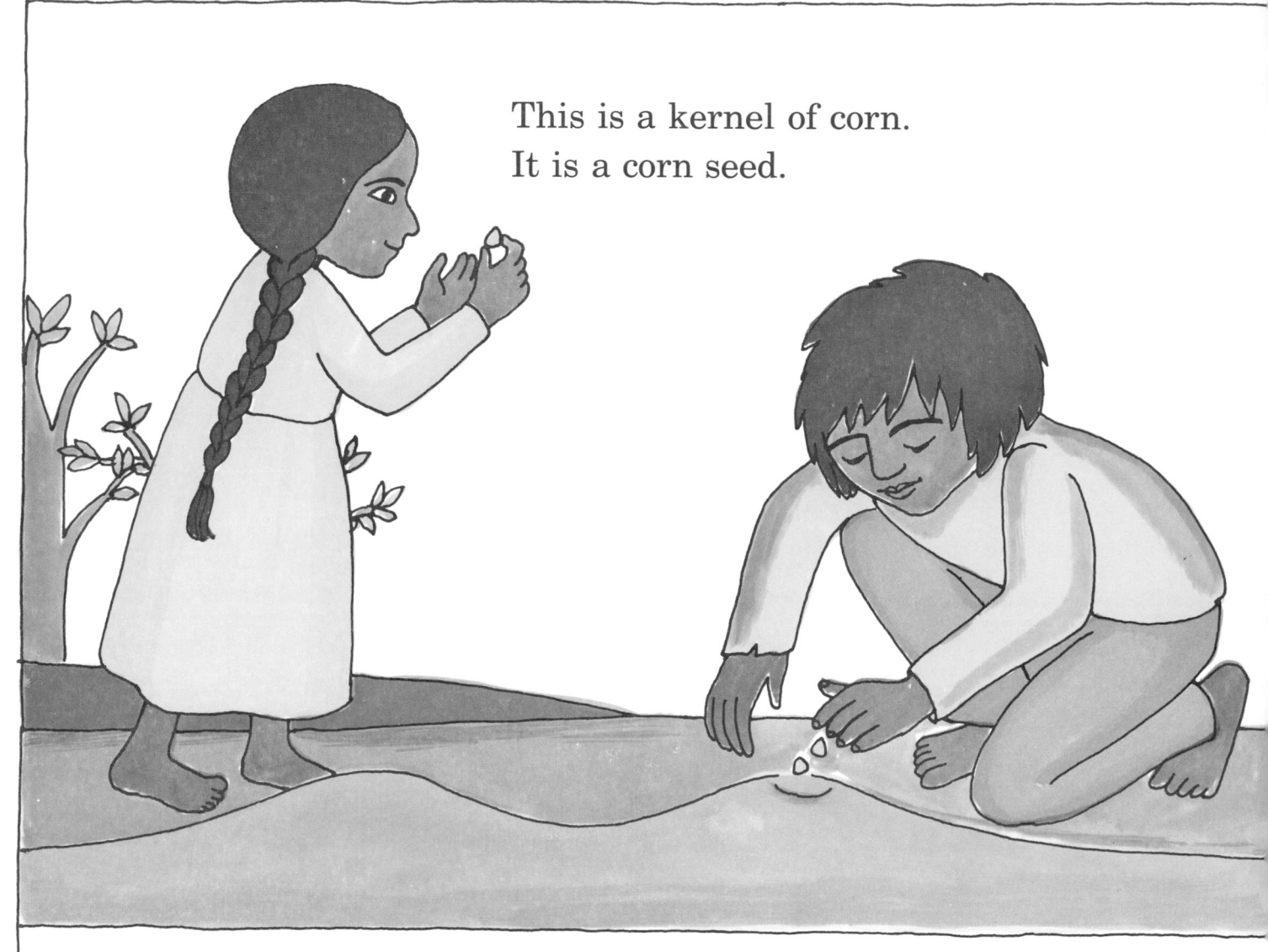

Kernels of corn are planted in a small hill of good earth.

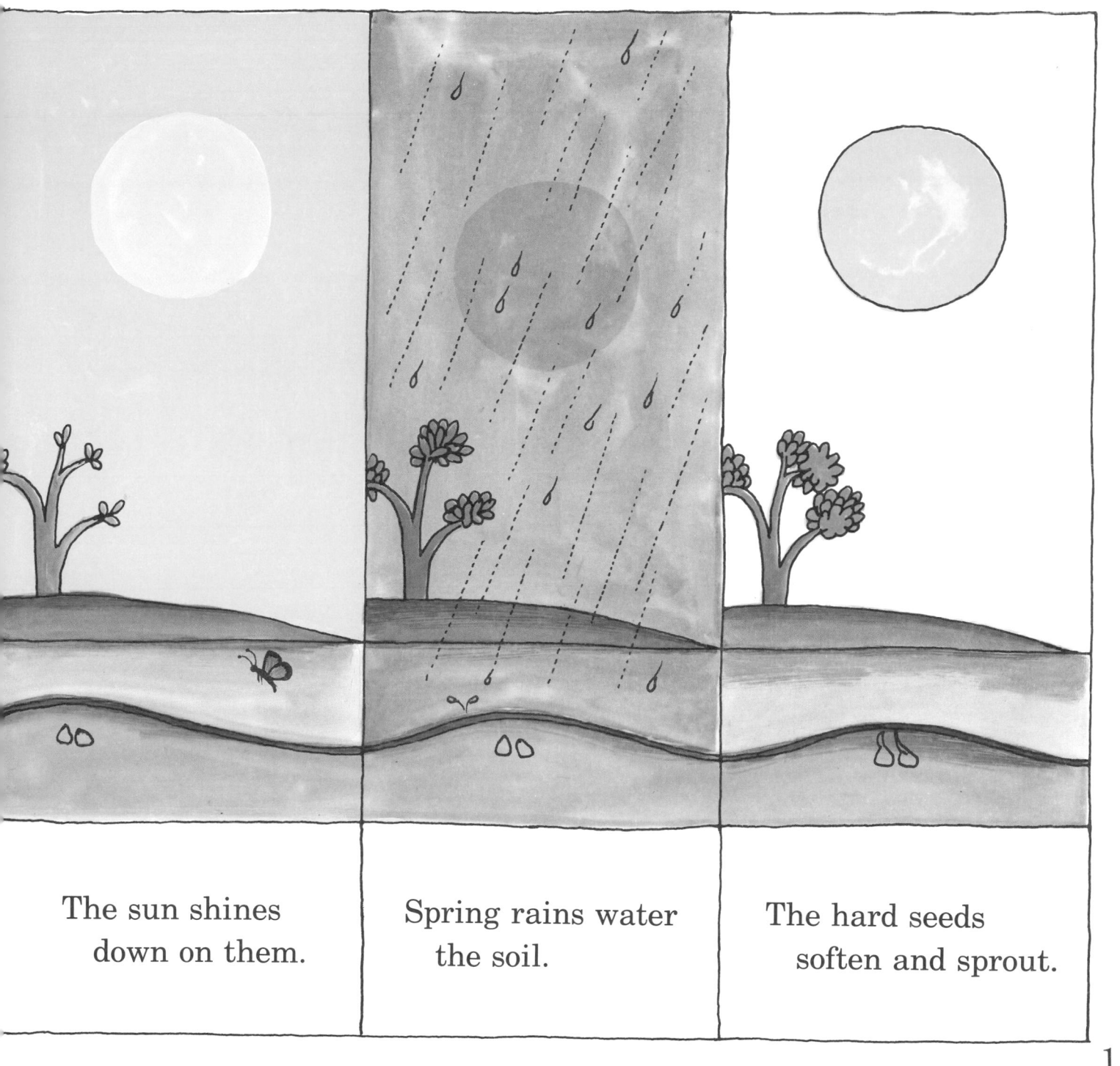

| The sun shines down on them. | Spring rains water the soil. | The hard seeds soften and sprout. |

1

A leaf appears
and a stalk
begins to grow.

More leaves
come from joints
called nodes.

A corn stalk
shoots up fast.
Farmers say that
on a quiet evening
they can hear
the corn growing.

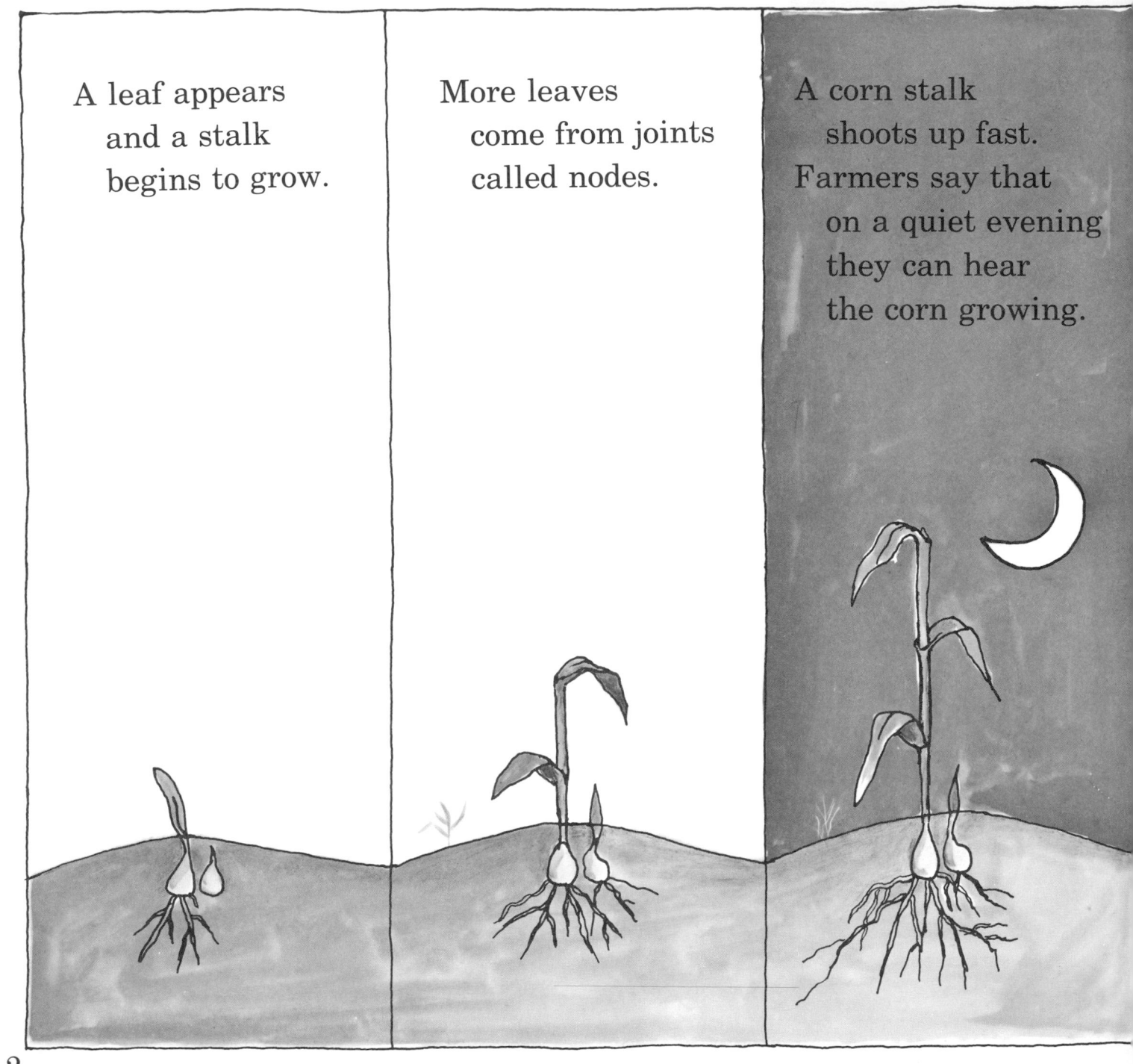

By midsummer, the plant is taller than a farmer.
Husks have begun to sprout from the nodes.
A husk is a bundle of leaves tightly wrapped
  around strands of silk.
The corn silk is the female part of the plant.
Tassels grow like a hat at the top of the stalk.
The tassels are the male flowers.

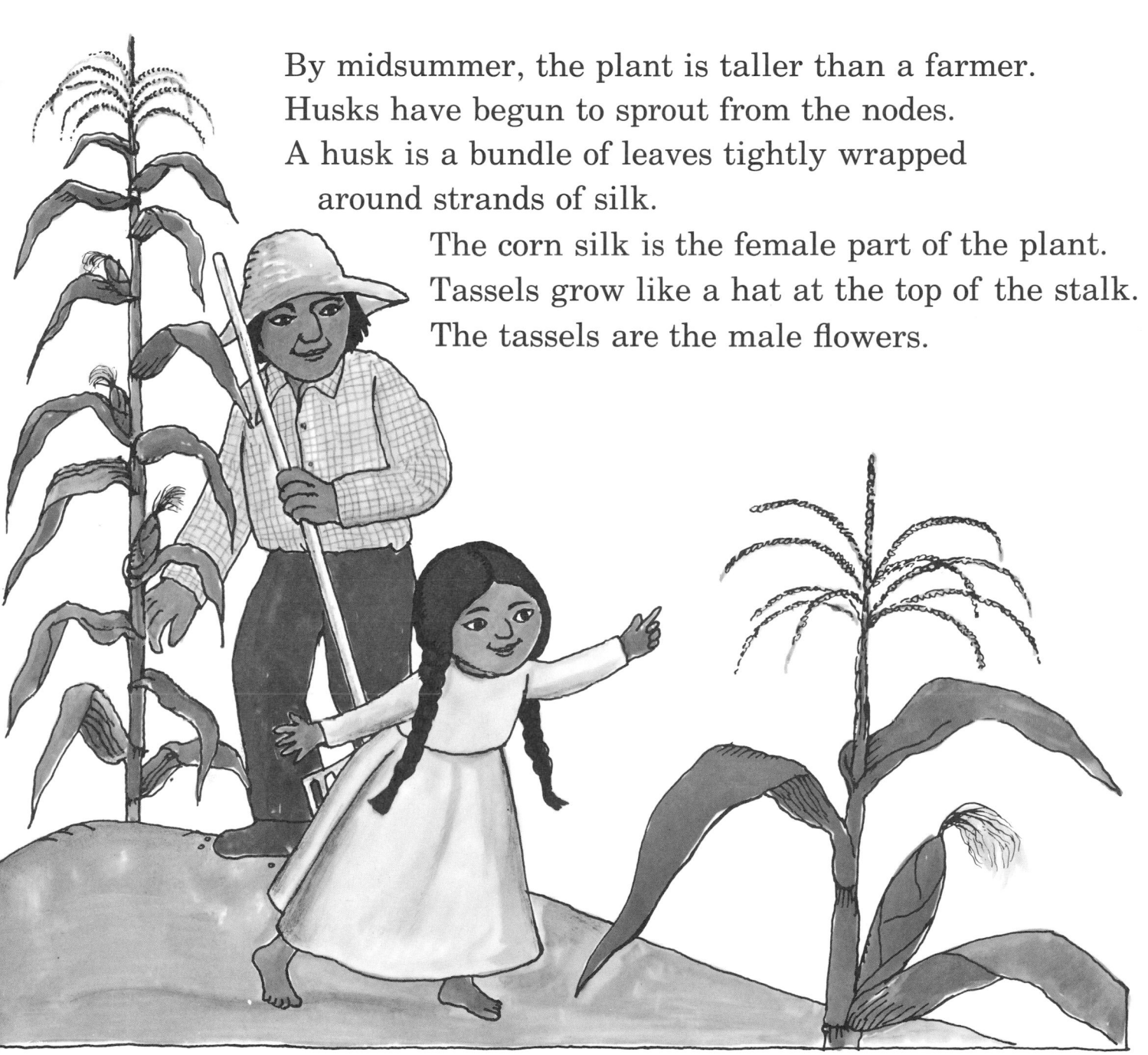

In the summer breeze, clouds of tiny grains
of pollen blow from the tassels.
The pollen falls on the silk of neighboring corn plants.
Each pollen grain pollinates the strand of silk it sticks to.
After fertilization, a kernel of corn will grow at the
end of each strand.

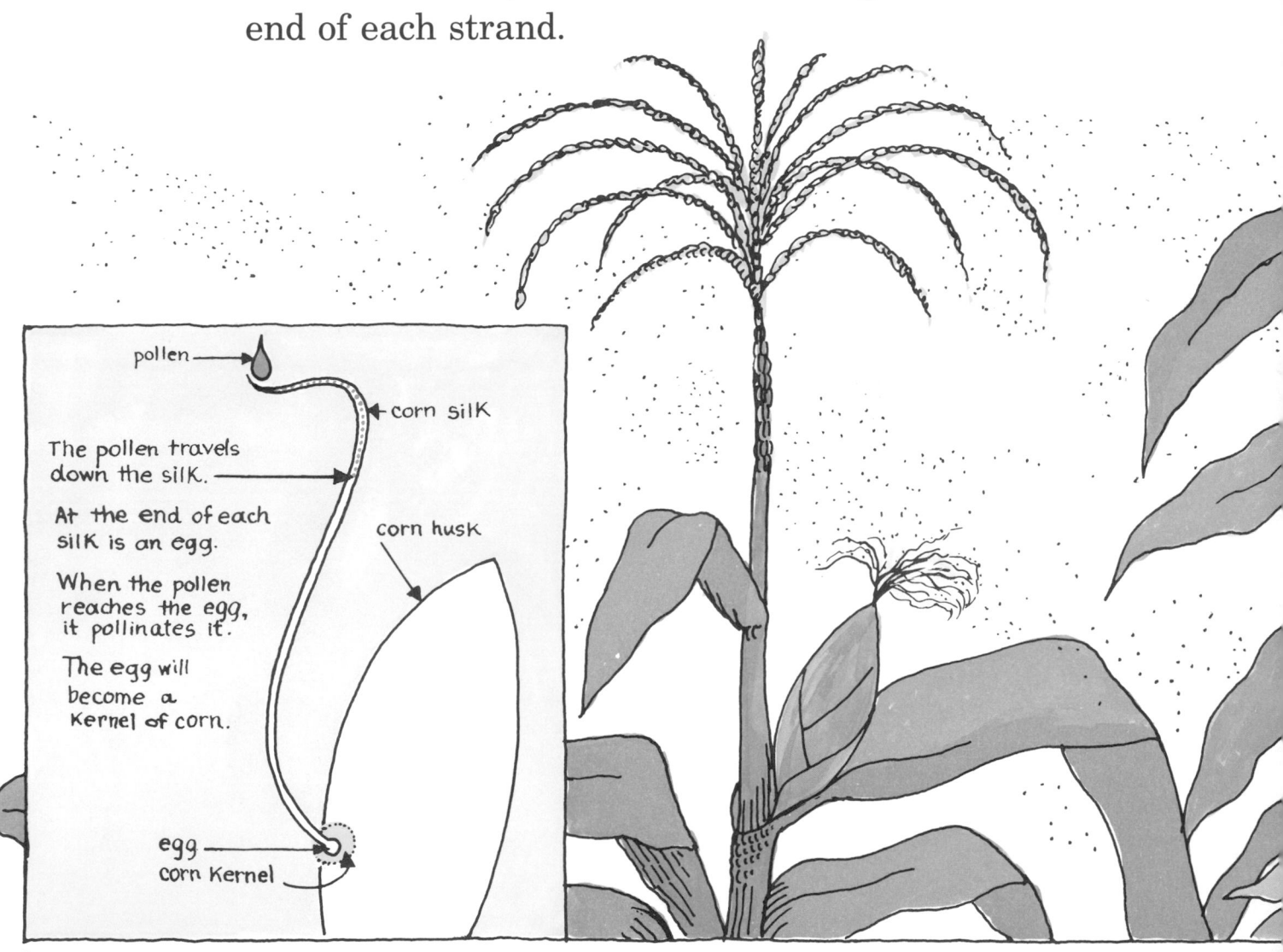

pollen

corn silk

The pollen travels
down the silk.

At the end of each
silk is an egg.

corn husk

When the pollen
reaches the egg,
it pollinates it.

The egg will
become a
Kernel of corn.

egg
corn Kernel

The corn husk grows.
Inside the wrapped leaves, hundreds of
   kernels grow into an ear of corn.
The silk turns from a creamy color to
   dark red to brown.

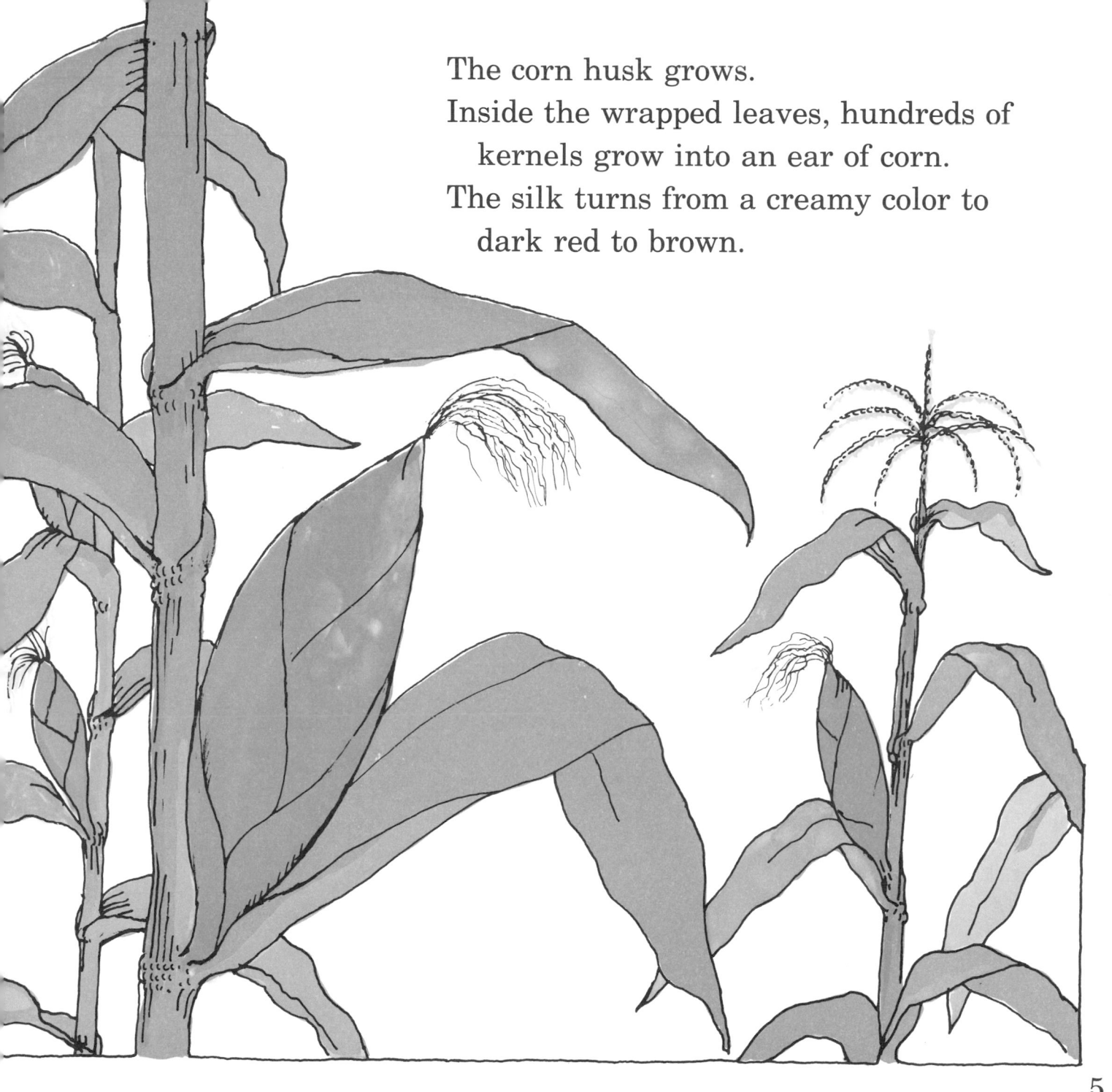

Just before it turns brown, it is time to pick
the corn and husk it.
The husks and the silk are pulled away.
The sweet, juicy ear of corn is ready
to cook and eat.

Farmers leave some ears on the stalk.
The brown silk dries.
The kernels harden and are saved.
They are seeds for the next crop.

7

Many plants can grow wild.
The wind scatters their seeds over
the earth and they can grow.

Corn kernels cannot fly off the ear
and scatter.
If an ear fell to the ground, a sprout
would grow from each kernel.
The new sprouts would grow in a
tangled heap and die.

Corn cannot grow by itself.
Corn seeds must be planted so there is space around
each hill for the tall plants to grow.
The plants must be weeded or the baby sprouts
will be choked.
Corn cannot grow without the help of man.

Then where did corn come from?
How did it start?
For many years there was no answer.
It was a mystery.

Scientists knew corn belongs to the same
grain family as wheat, rye, oats, barley, and rice.
They are all grass plants.
They all have jointed stems and nodes.
They all grow wild.
But although scientists searched, they had
never found any wild corn.

wheat

rye

oats

barley

rice

Not long ago they found some.
It was in a cave in Mexico where people once lived.
They found scraps of plants and tiny ears of
    ancient corn, more than 5,000 years old.
It was not like any the scientists had ever seen.

At last they could piece together the story of
how corn began.

Thousands of years ago, people lived in caves
in South and Central America.
They planted the seeds of a wild grass,
perhaps one found in the cave.

Teosinte growing wild.

Scientists think the ancient plant was a tall stalk
with one ear at the top.
The tassel grew out of the ear.
Each tiny orange or brown kernel was wrapped in
its own husk or pod.
The kernels grew so loosely they could fall off the
cob and plant themselves.
The cave dwellers planted and cared for this pod corn.

In time, some scientists think, the pollen of
another grass, called teosinte, or pollen of other
plants, fertilized the corn.
It took hundreds of years for the plants to grow
stronger and the ears larger.

Pollen of other plants and teosinte mixed with pod corn to make bigger and bigger ears of corn.

People found the grain was good for them.
It made them stronger than just beans, squash,
   and other plants they knew about.

Tribes in the north began to grow corn, too.
In time, people in all the Americas were growing
   different kinds.
They learned the right time to plant according
   to their climate.

Different tribes planted in different ways.
Some tribes planted five seeds in a hill.
Others planted two.
Some tribes planted bean seeds with the corn
   kernels so the vine could grow up the stalk.
Many tribes learned to bury a fish in each hill.
The fish rotted and made good soil.

By the time Christopher Columbus landed in the New World,
  the people he named "Indians" were expert farmers.
The women tended the crops while the men hunted.
They harvested the corn.
Some of it they ate fresh.
Most of it they dried.
They saved some for seed.
The rest they ground into meal on a
  flat stone called a metate.
They ate the meal dry or made bread with it.
They cooked it into mush.

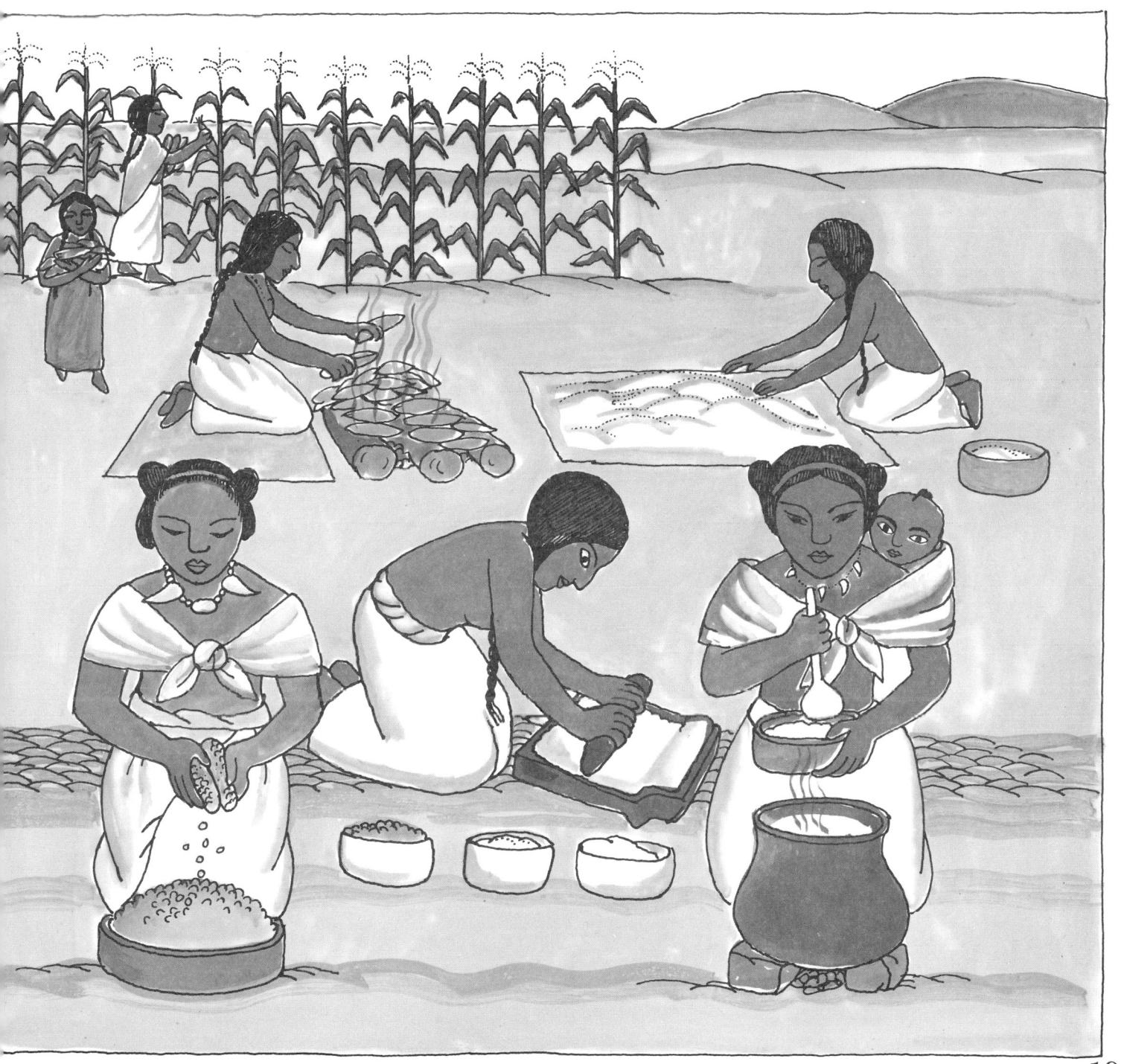

19

Indians of Mexico used cornmeal to make pancakes
 called tortillas.
They made tamales by wrapping spiced meat
 mixed with meal in husks and boiling them.

Many tribes boiled tiny, tender corn in the husks
 and ate the ears whole.
They ate corn on the cob.
They popped it.

Tribes in the north cooked corn with beans and
 called it misickquatash.
Indians ate the tassels of the corn plant and
 sucked the sweet, fresh stalks.

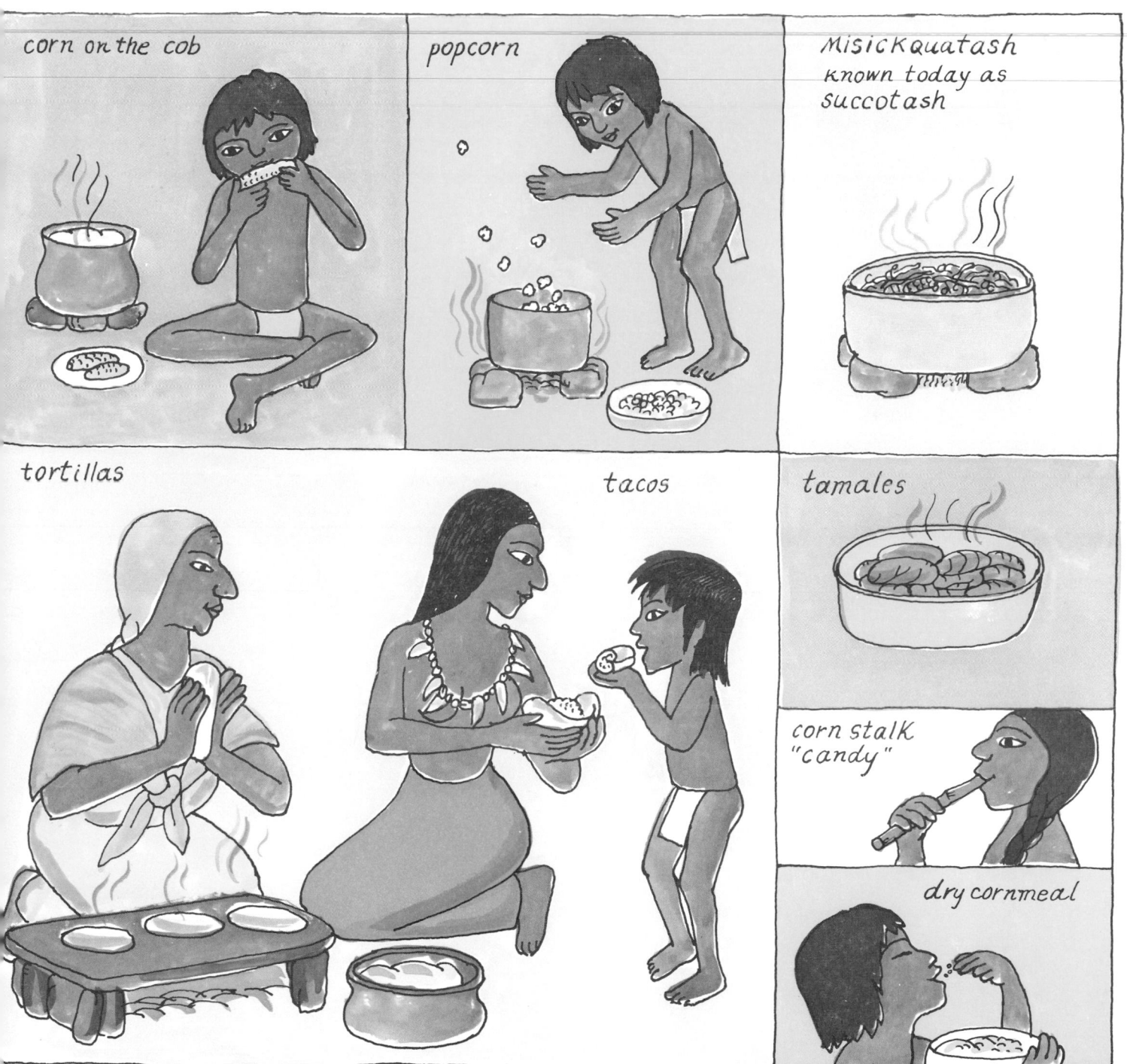

corn on the cob

popcorn

Misickquatash known today as succotash

tortillas

tacos

tamales

corn stalk "candy"

dry cornmeal

21

ashes
earth
grass

Hidatsa Indians stored
corn in the ground.

They learned to store corn for the
long winter ahead.
Corn, the Indians' only grain, was their main food.
Their lives depended on it.
Corn was so important to them, the various tribes
prayed to the Corn Gods they believed had
sent it to them.

Some Ancient Corn Gods

They had festivals at planting time and at harvest.
They chanted and made music, and each tribe
danced its own Corn Dance.

Pueblo Corn Dance of today

When Christopher Columbus returned to
Europe he told of the Indians
and the grain they grew.
He called it maize, which sounded
like the name the Indians had used.
Even today the correct word for
corn is maize.

The word "corn" means "grain."
Corn is also the word used for
the most important grain a
country grows.
In some countries wheat is called
corn.
In others, oats are called corn.
The Pilgrims called maize
"Indian corn," and Americans
have called it corn ever since.

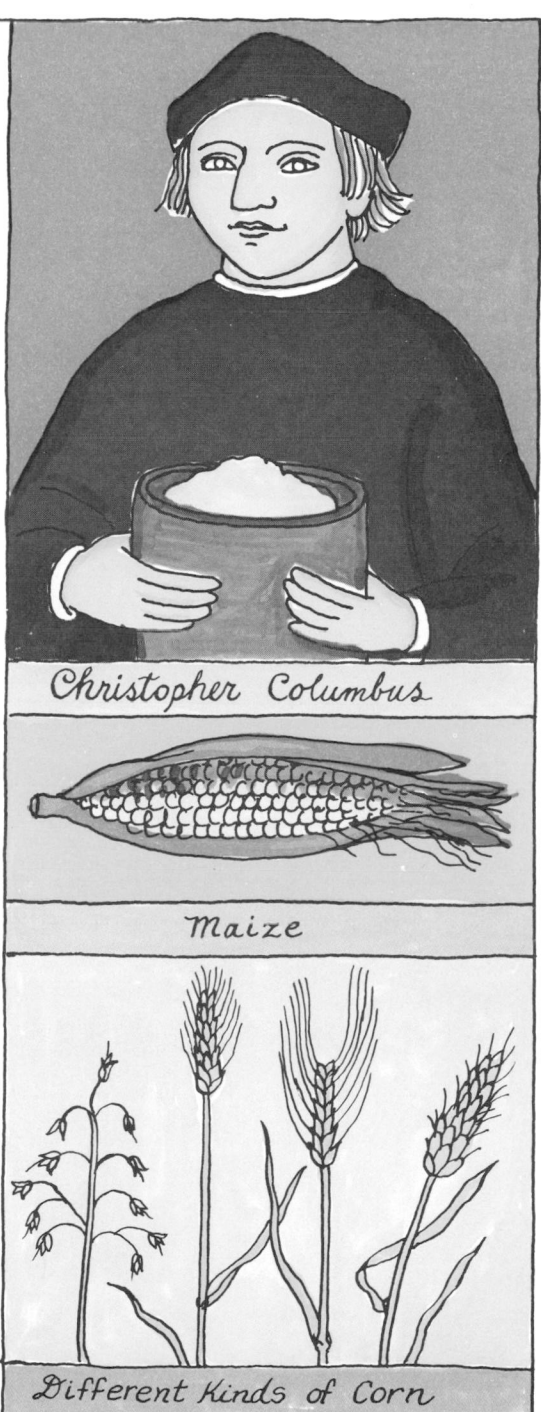

Christopher Columbus

Maize

Different Kinds of Corn

When the Pilgrims landed in America, maize saved
their lives.
Indians gave them the dried grain to eat and
showed them how to plant the crop.

On the first Thanksgiving, the Pilgrims and the
Indians together gave thanks for the corn
harvest, as the Indians had done long before.

The Pilgrims learned other things from the Indians.
They stuffed mattresses with husks, burned cobs for fuel,

made corncob pipes and corn-shuck dolls, too.

Today people all over the world grow corn.
There are many, many kinds.

Here are some:

pop · sweet · flour · flint · dent · pod

We eat only sweet corn, and use popcorn for popping.
The rest is used to feed animals and to make:

| corn flour | cornmeal | cornstarch | corn oil | corn syrup | cereal |
| baby powder | glue | soap | alcohol | medicine | ..and many other things. |

28

Now scientists have developed new kinds of corn
  that have more and better protein than any other kind.

People need protein to make them strong and healthy.
Scientists hope someday this new corn will
  help many hungry people in the world.

Harvester

On large farms today machines help farmers plow
and sow seeds.
A harvester picks corn and dries it so it can be
stored without rotting.
Then it is taken to a mill to be ground.

old gray goose

seeds

miller

millstone

flour

farmer bringing corn seeds

waterwheel

This is an early mill, run by water.
Today mills are run by electricity.

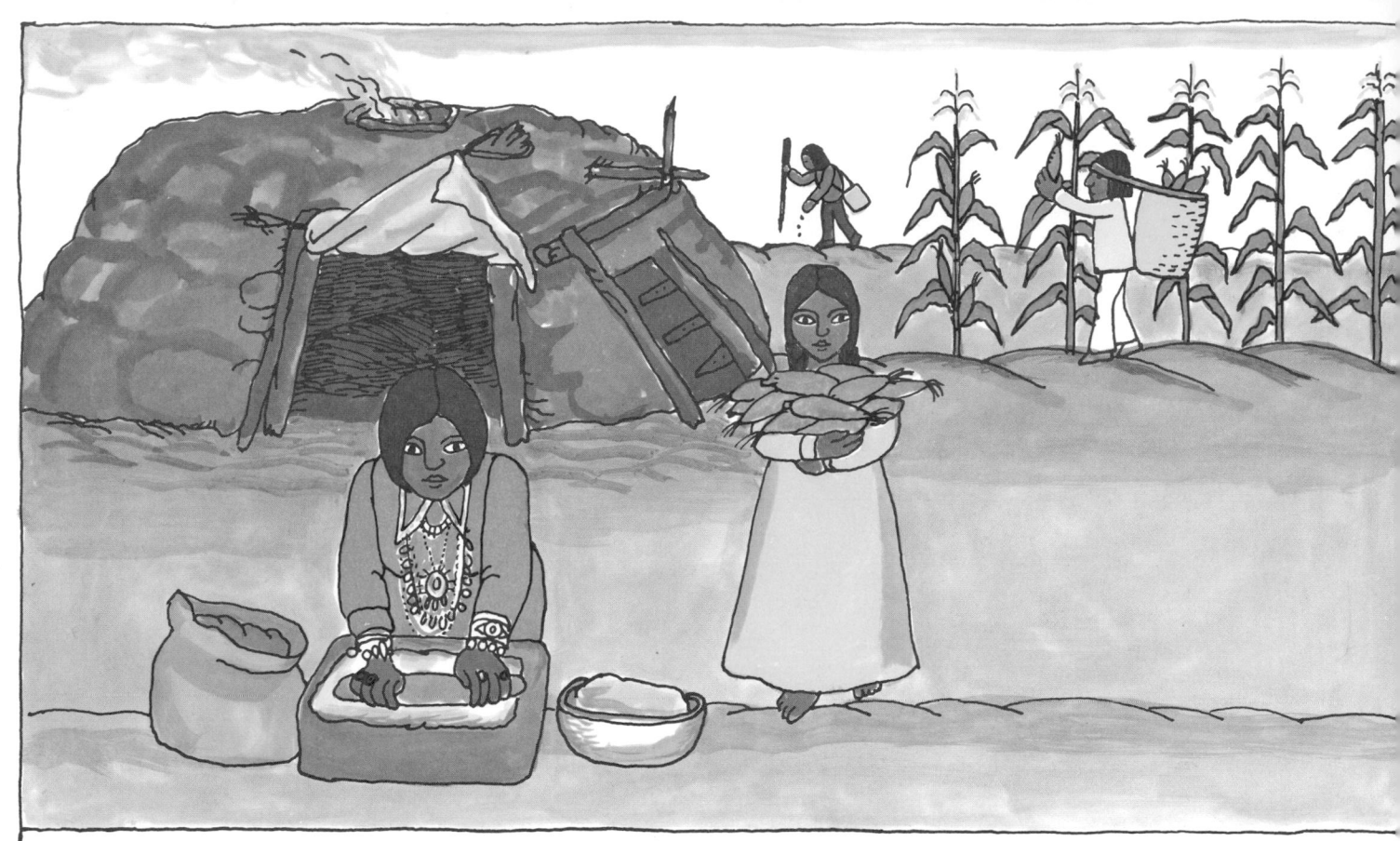

But not all corn is planted and ground by machines.
In parts of America, Indian farmers still grow their corn.
They plant the seeds as their ancestors once did.
They care for the plant, harvest it, and grind
  it on a metate.

And they praise the corn that has fed
their people for thousands of years.

ALIKI'S CORN HUSK DOLL

ABOUT THE AUTHOR-ILLUSTRATOR

Aliki Brandenberg has been fascinated by corn ever since she took her first bite and felt the butter drip down her arm. She also has a great interest in American Indians, their culture and art. In this book, both subjects are brought together.

Mrs. Brandenberg often treats her family to corn fritters, corn bread, and other corn dishes. Then, being a person who throws nothing away, she makes dolls and wreaths with the husks.

Aliki grew up in Philadelphia and was graduated from the Philadelphia College of Art. She now lives in London with her husband in the winter, and spends summers in Switzerland and Greece and other countries where corn grows.

ALIKI'S CORN HUSK WREATH

1. Bend a wire hanger.

2. Fold one fresh husk (a) and tie it over hanger (b and c). Repeat and repeat. When wire is full—

3. —use pin to shred. Let it dry.

4. Finished wreath.